1,000,000 Books

are available to read at

---◊---

www.ForgottenBooks.com

---◊---

**Read online
Download PDF
Purchase in print**

ISBN 978-0-259-38213-3
PIBN 10814762

1 MONTH OF
FREE
READING

at

www.ForgottenBooks.com

By purchasing this book you are eligible for one month membership to ForgottenBooks.com, giving you unlimited access to our entire collection of over 1,000,000 titles via our web site and mobile apps.

To claim your free month visit:
www.forgottenbooks.com/free814762

English
Français
Deutsche
Italiano
Español
Português

www.forgottenbooks.com

Mythology Photography **Fiction**
Fishing Christianity **Art** Cooking
Essays Buddhism Freemasonry
Medicine **Biology** Music **Ancient**
Egypt Evolution Carpentry Physics
Dance Geology **Mathematics** Fitness
Shakespeare **Folklore** Yoga Marketing
Confidence Immortality Biographies
Poetry **Psychology** Witchcraft
Electronics Chemistry History **Law**
Accounting **Philosophy** Anthropology
Alchemy Drama Quantum Mechanics
Atheism Sexual Health **Ancient History**
Entrepreneurship Languages Sport
Paleontology Needlework Islam
Metaphysics Investment Archaeology
Parenting Statistics Criminology
Motivational

The Christian Sun.

In Essentials—Unity, in Non-Essentials—Liberty, in All Things—Charity.

ESTABLISHED 1844. GREENSBORO N. C., WEDNESDAY, August 12, 1908 VOLUME LX. NUMBER 33.

All communications, whether for publication or pertaining to matters of. business, should be sent to the Editor, J. O. Atkinson, Elon College, N. C.

EDITORIAL COMMENT.

The Czar Learning. The first assembly of the Russian Douma was precipitately prorogued by the Emperor and sent home. Maybe that was well for if was a bad lot. It was too fiery, too reckless, and radical.

The present one is of better stuff and seems destined to a better fate. The members are of broader mind and build, and seem to know what they were elected for, and what their country needs. The Czar is hearing them and is on fairly friendly terms. During the last month the Douma has appropriated nearly five million dollars for general improvement, and the Czar has expressed complete satisfaction and approval. There have been army and navy laws and regulations suggested and some passed, of which the Emperor approves. The Czar of all the Russias is learning that with growing intelligence the masses love and demand self-government, and that they may be trusted. Russia is waking up.

Some More Facts. The masses learn facts and figures slowly—if it all. The average man will put his own observations, it matters not how limited, up against the most authentic statistics any time. And when general, and universal, facts conflict with one's own experience, the facts simply do not count. According to the Chief of Police of Atlanta, Georgia, tabulated statistics show that for the first three months of 1908, under prohibition, the number of arrests fell from 5,277 to 2,010, a decrease over the previous year of 3,267. And for drunkenness there were only 323 arrests against 1,293 arrests of the corresponding quarter under the open saloon. The Chief further declares that there have been "fewer complaints of severe distress among the poor and more cash for household expenses."

If facts and figures could count and convince, prohibition would have long since swept this country. But they do not count against "what a man sees with his own eyes and hears with his own ears." So we have no doubt but that hundreds, yes thousands, of people in Atlanta would tell you that prohibition was "no good"—facts or no facts.

The Denominational College.—Just now hundreds of fathers are debating about sending their sons and daughters to college. It is no easy matter to decide. Destiny often hinges on this decision. The child's future certainly very largely depends upon it.

Such a field opens up unlimited discussion. This page could be easily filled with our own thoughts and ideas. But there are too or three opinions at hand which we regard so weighty that we give place to them. They are worth considering.

Dr. James M. Buckly, editor of New York Christian Advocate, writes:

"The future life of a student depends very much upon the spirit that becomes second nature to him while in college. If spiritual religion departs from him (if it ever existed in him) during that period, and he goes out in the world filled with other thoughts, even though they be not antagonistic, there will be little room for the impressions and internal suggestions which determine the relation of their possessor to church life and to the more important spiritual ife. The Roman Catholics are extremely wise in inducing as many as they can of their members to go to their own institutions. By that they culminate a long course of training that began in the cradle. When they go to other institutions a greater degree of interest in the students seems to be manifest by local priests than is sometimes the case in Protestant denominations. To send a boy to an institution wholly antagonistic to the faith of his fathers is a contradiction. * * * When a father has to decide to what college his son shall go he should not rely on advertisements or denominational relations merely, but should visit the institution, if possible, or make the most careful inquiries as to whether a religious spirit exists and a proper regard is paid to the developing, moral and religious character of the students. Better send a boy a thousand miles to a college pervaded with a religious spirit (provided it does not depend upon the religious spirit to cover its intellectual poverty), if such an institution can be found at that distance, than to send him but twenty miles away to one where the sole object is educating the intellect."

President Angell, of the University of Michigan, is quoted as saying:

"I am inclined to think that most of the State universities are suffering from excessive attendance. It is apparent to me that one of the greatest problems before the universities of the nation during the next twenty years will be how to administer these rapidly growing institutions properly."

The Chicago Record-Herald says:

"The day of the smaller college is coming again. Of course the special inducements offered by State universities as public institutions will always make them popular, but may there not be some relief because of the preference which many people now express for small colleges? The country has scores of these colleges, and not a few of them enjoy an excellent reputation. They can have as fine a discipline as many of the larger institutions, have the advantage of bringing faculty and students close together and are freer from distractions than the big rivals. * * * A professor in one of those vast State institutions told us some time ago that he would never entrust his son to it for training. To our question as to the ground for this strange remark, he said oracularly: 'The gains are too little and the possible losses too great. I prefer the smaller college.'"

Good reports come from many quarters of successful revivals in the churches. There is no news more gratifying than that of gracious revivals, the conversion of souls and the building up of the kingdom.

Rev. J. S. Carden assisted Pastor S. B. Klapp in a glorious revival at Pleasant Ridge, Guilford County, last week, there being twenty-three conversions and the church much revived. Bro. Carden is this week assisting Rev. T. W. Strowd in a meeting at Center Grove.

LIFE IN CHRIST.
By Rev. D. E. Millard, D. D.

Jesus says to his believing disciples—"I. give unto them eternal life, and they never shall perish. I am the resurrection and the life. My words they are spirit and they are life." The soul-renewed Christian knows the full import of this language and feels ite power. He can say with Paul, "I am crucified with Christ, nevertheless I live; yet not I, but Christ liveth in me, and the life which I now live in the flesh, I live by faith in the Son of God."

A Christian at heart is not a figure simply, for that wants life. He is a living character, possessing all the traits of life. He can say with assurance—I live, I eat the bread of life, and drink the water of life: I feel the pulse of sacred emotions beat; I breathe the breath of prayer. I put forth exertions, and although they show weakness, they bespeak life. Jesus is the bread of life. With Him is life, without Him all, all is death.

And how emphatic are the claims of Christ. He always claims power to impart more than his teachings or example, even the direct quickening of his own spiritual life, the higher vitality of his spiritual being. "He that believeth in me, though he were dead, yet shall he live: and whosoever liveth and believeth in me shall never die." He constantly affirms that, for the sustenance and full development of the germs of eternal life within us, it is as essential to assimilate to our spirits the divine elements of his moral and spiritual nature, as it is needful, physically, to assimilate material substance to our bodily organism in order that animal existence may be maintained.

The divine life was the center and soul of Christ's existence. This life was evermore revealed through him. It was the source of his words and the soul of his deeds. It was the divine attraction that drew to him his earliest followers. They could not discern all the greatness of his glory; but as rain and sun and air quicken the torpid and unconscious seed, so his divine influence caused them to grow. That influence entered their souls, subordinated and transformed the earthly elements within them, and caused them finally to stand forth as new men in Christ.

This life, sweet, sacred, and mighty as it had been on earth, was finally concentrated and exalted in his death. Saul of Tarsus who had sat at the feet of Gamaliel, had lived a zealous Pharisee, had been present as a consenting party to the death of Stephen, had departed on his way to persecute the church at Damascus, saw in a vision and in a light from heaven the Divine Image that had so impressed, illumined, and ennobled those who had been brought within his power during its sojourn upon earth; and forthwith the sacred presence, remaining evermore in his secret conscientiousness, pervaded, converted, inspired and made its own, the fiery but noble-minded persecutor—wrought and finally completed a new life within him, changing him into his own image from glory to glory. And such changes he has continued to work from that day to this. He is still the bread of life, and communicates the life that is in him to hearts open to receive it. "Lord, evermore give us this bread!"

Portland, Mich.

PRINCIPLES OF CHRISTIANITY.
What Is Christianity?

Before answering this question I submit the following fundamental definitions, gathered and condensed from various sources. Religion is the life of God in the soul of man. This life manifests itself in the sinner in a Godly sorrow for sin, fellowship with God because of the forgiveness of sin, and a new and divine life became of the redemption from sin. Doctrine is what we think about religion. Theology is the reason for religion. The church is religion organized. Religion is natural to man and universal among men. It is natural for man to appeal to the unknown power above him; bow to the unseen authority, and seek after the invisible fellowship about him. The Christian religion is the thought, feelings, and institutions that have resulted from the influence of Jesus on the religious life of mankind.

Christianity, then, is Christ—the blossom and fruit of His life. It is spirit of God as the pure river of the water of life clear as crystal, proceeding out of the throne of God and of the Lamb purifying humanity as it courses down the ages. Roll on, thou Jordan, roll until the perfection God shall cover the earth as the waters cover the sea.

Christianity is a life—a birth from above. It is a man in Christ, and Christ in the man. The life such a man lives in the flesh he lives by the faith that was in the Son of God. The same life principle by which Christ lived in the sinless and holy life is the principle by which he lives and becomes perfect even as his Father in Heaven is perfect. The same over-shadowing power that made Mary the mother of Jesus forms Christ in us, thus making us heirs with God and joint heirs with His Son.

Christianity is the science of right living. It teaches us that we should live soberly in relation to ourselves and the things about us; that life does not consist in the abundance of the things we possess; that things are made for man, and not man for things; that we should use anything that makes us better and nothing that injures us, or is a cause of stumbling to others; that the soul of improvement is in the improvement of the soul. It teaches us that we should live rightly in relation to our fellowman; that we are brothers through the fatherhood of God; that justice is the golden rule of brotherhood—doing unto others as we would have them do unto us; that all wealth is common wealth—our possessions are a public trust; that he who would rule must be servant of all; that all who love serve all who suffer; that the love that does not love enemies is not love. It teaches us that we should live Godly in relation to the God above us; that we should not misrepresent or slander the God and Father of Jesus Christ; that to know Christ is to know God; that to believe on Christ is to live His life; that to be saved is to be a partaker of the divine nature; that the future life is a continuation of this life.—R. E. Peele, in News and Observer.

COMMERCIALISM.

What is it? We once heard an eminent preacher say that he could not define commercialism, but he could tell what it suggested to his mind—"a silver dollar turned on edge and set a rolling, and a hundred men after it in hot pursuit and jostling each other in the race." It is said the spirit of commercialism is growing more intense, the chase of the dollar more strenuous, year after year. Especially is this true in the South, and this is accounted for by the rapid development of our material resources. As these develop, fortunes are made more rapidly and more easily. Increase of riches stimulates the greed of gain. "Much wants more."

Moreover, when one man gets rich, his neighbors are spurred on. When one plans his living on a more expensive style, others are tempted to imitate. One automobile begets another. Luxuries soon come to be rated as necessities. Costlier living creates a demand for a larger income. More money must be had, and then still more money must be had; thus the race after the dollar grows ever more earnest, more eager, more exciting.

This commercial spirit is telling on our education. It insists that education must be intensely practical, exclusively utilitarian. It builds technological schools, and puts to the front the arts and sciences that bear directly on industrial pursuits. Dominated by the commercial spirit, parents send their children to school as an investment. The prime aim is to increase their earning capacity, to have them trained into expert money-getters. "How much better it is to get understanding than to get gold," said Solomon. The modern Solomon says, "How much better it is to get the kind of understanding that will help you to get gold." Getting understanding is but a means to getting gold. The end is gold, the natural object of civilized man's idolatry.

The commercial spirit is threatening to tell on our education in a different way. A financial inducement of a very tempting kind is offered to break the alliance, where such alliance exists, between education and the church. The design seems to be to free education from religious influence. Denominational institutions as a rule are poor. The salaries which they are able to pay are small. Those, whose bread and meat are dependent on these salaries, have before them the alternative of premature death, or an old age of poverty. They can lay up little or nothing for the rainy day. It would make their position much more agreeable if they could look forward to an honorable retirement on a comfortable pension. Just this change could be effected by removing the institution from church control. How strong the temptation! Too strong to be resisted in many quarters.

Teaching talent, like other talent, is on the market. It is usually put up for the highest bidder. The church institution is put at a disadvantage. The pension fund has raised the bid of its competitors. The silver dollar on edge is rolling away from the college with a religious aim, the college tied to the church. Every man who has consecrated his life to teaching is called on to decide another question of consecration. Is his ideal to make money, or to mould manhood? Is it to catch the dollar, or to create character?

The commercial spirit has invaded the sphere of education; and the time is near at hand, if it is not already here, when one of two things must happen, if the church is not to see the higher education pass entirely from her control: either the sons of the church who have money must put it at the service of the church so that it can bid the highest market price for talent, or the sons of the church who have the talent must rise to that height of religious consecration where they can serve Christ at a sacrifice. "Ye cannot serve God and Mammon" is coming to mean for the teacher, "ye cannot serve God and secure a pension."—Presbyterian Standard.

SUMMER SUNDAYS.

All Chirstians in good health, not detained by sickness of others in the home or by some other bona fide duty, should attend the public service of God at least once on the Sabbath. Those situated where there is no church have excellent opportunity to promote some form of religious service. One of the best ways of doing this (after consultation with others) is to secure if possible some one to read a selection from the Scriptures, offer prayer, and introduce well-known hymns. If individuals or Christian families are in a village or hotel beyond the "sound of the Sabbath bell," it would be strange if an interesting social and service could not be provided.

It is a peculiar aberration of judgment, if nothing worse, for professed Christians, who at home would be ashamed to remain away from the sanctuary without a cause that would be sufficient in the forum of conscience, to spend some weeks or perhaps the whole summer in the country without attending upon church. It would not be unjust to infer that no serious prayer is offered to God for direction on the Sabbath when such neglects take place. It implies an entirely worldly view of the Sabbath service and religious experience.

To substitute excursions in the woods, on the mountain, or along the streams, imagining that one is worshiping God by looking at His works, is one of those delusions which self-indulgence can spin more swiftly than any spider ever spins its web. The spider, however, catches something else; the wanderer from the house of God to His material works entangles his own soul.

To those who remember that God said, "From one Sabbath to another, shall all flesh come to worship before me," and "Not forsaking the assembling of yourselves together, as the manner of some is," the trees, the mountains and the streams will be not less beautiful, and a music sweeter than that of rivulets, the "music of a good conscience," will make the day twice blessed.

Ministers who turn their backs upon churches, and spend the Sabbath day in mere pleasure, in sitting upon hotel steps and chatting, are not only giving "occasion' to the enemies of the Lord to blaspheme," but leading astray lambs of the flock and confirming those who are like-minded with them in their contumelious treatment of the house of God.

Each year we hear of the good done by city pastors and laymen at the summer resorts, and also the evil done by others.

Since writing the above a letter has come from the pastor of country church in a delightful region. Mournfully he notes that "the time of the invasion of our country by our city cousins is upon us, and, alas! country pastors regard it with sinking hearts. Though the majority of these visitors are probable church members and atttend church, some of them being very active when at home, here they do not attend church, and, what is worse for the church in that neighborhood, they keep the residents at home waiting on them, and instead of the congregation being strengthened and inspired by their visit among us, as it should be, the very opposite is the case."

He concludes his letter, however, in a more cheerful vein by describing a "rare exception." A wealthy Presbyterian family have a summer residence in a wild but beautiful region. The family consists of the parents, four boys and a servant. When they are in the country they do not forget their religion: Every Sunday they load themselves, servant and all, into a huge wagon and, there being no church of their own persuasion near, drive four miles to a little Baptist church, attending the morning service and Sunday school.

Many country churches are doubtless fading away. Several causes contribute to this condition, but one of the most pernicious of those elements of destruction is the Sabbath conduct of visitors from the cities, and in particular the inconsistency of professed Christians.

It is difficult to believe that those who thus treat the day and the sanctuary, when at home can be active in a spiritual way. That phrase "active in church work" has divers meanings, and the number of them grows with the ever-increasing enterprises undertaken by the local church.—N. Y. Christian Advocate.

THE LARGEST GIVER.

I want to tell you of an inquiry of my little five-year-old Helen. She attends Sunday school regularly. Returning home one Sunday, she said:

"Mama, every Sunday the man reads how much money each class gives, and then he tells how much Total gives, and Total gives more than anyone. He must be a rich man. Who is Total, mama?"
—The September Delineator.

It is given out that at least $50,000 will be necessary to conduct the Democratic presidential campaign, and we suppose equally so much will be needed by the Republicans. Campaigns are expensive because of postage, printing, secretaries and speakers, but they are educational, and do much to enlighten the masses in matters political and civic.

NOTES AND PERSONALS.

It was to be expected. England is now planning a still bigger ship, one of 21,000 tons, and Admiral Evans says that the 25,000-ton ship is coming. Perhaps before that the nations will come to their senses.

From a Texas farm the other day about four tons of live rattlesnakes, worth about ten thousand dollars, were shipped to various circuses and museums. Before shipment their fangs were removed and all were harmless.

Rev. G. R. Underwood recently closed a good and successful meeting at Christian Chapel, he writes, in which revival the church was strengthened and the kingdom enlarged. Rev. J. S. Carden assisted in the good work.

Both Mr. Bryan and Mr. Taft have made campaign speeches to the graphophone. Each record is said to contain about 300 words. Soon we may all hear the voices of the presidential candidates —whether we see their faces or not.

Pastor R. P. Crumpler was assisted in a series of meetings at Salem Chapel, Forsyth Co., last week by Rev. J. L. Foster. There were two accessions to the church. At the close of the meeting a deacon was ordained to office in the church.

"The great wave of prohibition which is spreading over the country has its best support from the medical profession." That is the striking statement of Dr. Henry O. Marcy, of Boston, ex-president of the American Medical Association.—Exchange.

The platform adopted by the National Wholesale Liquor Dealers' Association solemnly declares that the saloon has been compelled by the political activity of the Anti-Saloon League, and much against its will, to enter politics. Grins are in order.—Exchange.

Five hundred thousand Bibles and Testaments were sold or given away in China last year; Korea and Japan together taking half as many. In its 92 years' existence the American Bible Society has issued 82,316,323 copies, or portions, of our Holy Bible.

The report that Rev. B. F. Young prints this week from Lanett, Alabama, is full of interest and encouragement. Already Bro. Young has received 73 members this year and is still active in the work. His is evidently a busy life and God is using his efforts to the salvation of souls.

Theodore Roosevelt, Jr., has decided to be a miner, go to work at the bottom and work up. That is sensible, and here is a wish for the young man's success.

It is announced, seemingly authentically, that a Frenchman has invented a gun worked by electricity, and which can fire without powder and with no explosion, 1,200 bullets a minute.

Governor Glenn delivered an address on Missions before the Missionary Conference of the Southern Presbyterian Church in session at Montreat, N. C., last week. Governor Glenn "makes good" in public address, whatever be the topic assigned him, and he is at home in the pulpit as well as on the hustings.

United States Senator Allison, of Iowa, died of heart failure at his home in Dubuque Aug. 4. He was in his eightieth year. In 1863 he was elected to Congress; and in 1873 to the Senate, of which body he remained a conspicuous member till death—an unbroken period of 35 years. He had been in public life since 1860, a period of 48 years. A remarkable record.

Our Christian Sun printers have decided that Rev. D. A. Long, D.D., is the kindest hearted man, and most thoughtful, at large. Two large watermelons, a basket of peaches and grapes sent to the office force last Tuesday by Dr. Long tell the secret. And, my! how we all did enjoy them. It is devoutly desired that dear Dr. Long will live through many more summers, and may his like multiply in the earth, and his timely and generous thought be taken as a model.

In closing a personal letter to the editor the venerable and distinguished Rev. Thomas Holmes, D.D., LL.D., Chelsea, Mich., employs this splendid sentiment: "This is God's world and He is framing. Freedom of thought exercised by the masses, and directed by principles of righteousness and altruism—religion —are the means by which He will ultimately banish from the world both tyranny and anarchy.

"'Freedom and reason make us men.
Take these away, what are we then?
Mere animals, and just as well
The brutes may talk of heaven and
hell.'"

Rev. Edward Everett Hale has several appreciative studies in The Book News Monthly for August, Dr. Hale's own son, and Col. Thomas Wentworth Higginson, being among the contributors. This magazine grows in worth and interest every month and is certainly the magazine for those who wish to keep up with the new books and the literary trend. It is published by John Wanamaker, Philadelphia, and is ably edited, besides being artistically printed.

Our home county, Alamance, did herself proud last Thursday by voting with a substantial majority for the issuance of $200,000 fifty year five per cent bonds for the improvement of its public roads. This if judiciously spent means better travel in Alamance. Thus the cause of good roads gets another impetus which we trust will be felt in other sections. The rural districts of the Southern States have no greater need for rapid progress and improvement along all lines than this of better public highways. Good roads mean better farms, better schools, better churches, better citizens.

A WORD FROM PARIS.

Quite a contrast there is between Paris and her neighboring city across the channel. There is not the ease here, and Sabbath observance which one enjoys in London is entirely lacking. I feel like I am in an ungodly land. Sunday is the big day here. Shops are open, the bar-rooms and the many places of amusement thronged with people. The day of rest is made the day of amusement, the day of peace becomes the circus day. The theatre and music halls having afternoon performances on Sunday, races take place and almost all the great fetes on every Sunday. France indeed lives up to its catholic doctrines.

Paris well merits its reputation for gaity and, too, for music. Fashion plays here in full swing, the evening dinners and the swell balls are the fashionable features in Parisian society.

But of the more durable city there are many things to see. The city as a whole is beautiful, the shady streets, the many gardens, with flowers and gushing fountains, the palaces and mansions here and there, amongst lovely parks, present an ideal picture of a city. Notre Dame is the most ancient and most noted cathedral. It stands not far from the river, and the two flanking towers, 204 feet in height, and the colossal statue of Christ above the central door, give it an air of grandeur. Within its walls many scenes of history have been played, and here today one can see a nail and a piece of the Cross. The Empress Josephine and Napoleon were crowned here, in December 1804, and the robes they wore on that occasion are shown.

The Hotel de Cluny is one of the most noteworthy buildings in the city, both for its ancient architecture and its varied and valuable contents. Many royal personages sojourned here, amongst whom was Mary, the spirited princess and sister of Henry VIII who, after marrying the old king Louis XII to please her brother, left him and married the gallant Charles Brandon to please herself. The story is told in 'When knight-hood was in Flower.'

The most interesting place in Paris, as for art, is the Louvre. The building is in the form of a square around the large Cour du Louvre, looking upon the the Rue de Rivoli to the north and the Seine to the south. On the eastern front is the Colonnade, a fine series of fifty-two Corinthian pillars, in pairs. Within the gardens there is a fine statue of Lafayette, placed there by Americans. Within the palace, amongst the many interesting things, one sees the famous Venus of Milo. It is one of the masterpieces of ancient sculpture, and is said to be the most valued statue in the world.

In the Salle Chretienne are various memorials and monuments connected with the early days of Christianity. The coffin of Livia Primitiva, from Rome, is amongst the most ancient memorials of Christian times. Next to this is the Salle Judaique, containing antiquities connected with Palestine. Here you see coffins from the tombs of the kings; a monument of Herod; a Phoenician inscription recording the war of the Moabites against Israel at the death of Ahab, nearly 900 years before the Christian era; and many other things of no less interest.

In the different galleries are seen the bautiful paintings of Van Dyck, Rubens, David, Rembrandt, and others. The "Descent from the Cross," "Burial of Christ," the "Holy Family," and the "Nativity" are impressive. One cannot but be moved with admiration and love and reverence as he looks upon the life-like paintings of Christ's sufferings, death, and resurrection.

In the Pantheon, which is rather a civil temple, are the tombs of the well-known Mirabeau, Voltaire, Rousseau, and Victor Hugo.

The most visited place in Paris is no doubt the Hotel des Invalides where is seen the tomb of Napoleon. From the church floor, one looks down into the open crypt, and here exactly beneath the lofty dome, in a sarcophagus of red Finland granite, are deposited the remains of the great Napoleon. Just above the door of the crypt is inscribed the wish, as was well expressed in the Emperor's will:'je desire que mes cendres reposent sur les bords de la Seine, au milieu de ce peuple Francais, que jai tant aime.' And so does he repose upon the banks of the Seine, today, among those who now love his name, universally admired. The beautiful dome is 86 feet in diameter and the height to the summit of the Cross is 340 feet. It looks down upon the crypt and is divided into two sections. In the upper one is a statue of St. Louis offering to the Savior the sword with which he has fought for the Christian faith and in the lower are the statues of the apostles. The Emperor's tomb has a grandeur and a solemnity about it which I cannot express. The twelve colossal figures surrounding it and golden rays reflected upon it from the dome—this, the visible linked with the invisible, my admiration of the great military genius, made it the most impressive sight I have ever seen.

In the Hotel des Invalides are seen the saddle of Napoleon, swords, and other weapons of warfare. Also, here one sees the vault of General Bertrand, who accompanied the Emperor to St. Helena and remained faithful to him till his death, and Grouchy, to whose absence Napoleon ascribed the defeat of Waterloo.

The Place de la Bastille is interesting because of its association with French history—on the 14th of July, 1789, the 'fall of the Bastile' occurred. So that date is now a national holiday. Quite a celebration they had on this 14th—it was my '4th of July.'

Twelve miles southwest of Paris is situated the Palace of Versailles. Louis XIV was the original builder of the palace, and though since his time it has been largely added to and beautified. Before the palace in the center of the court-yard stands a large equestrian statue of Louis XIV. At this place assembled the Parisian rioters and the infuriated market women in 1789, clamoring for the heads of Louis XIV and his Austrian Queen, Marie Antoinette, who courageously went out on the balcony overlooking the great court-yard, taking her little boy in her arms, hoping by this appeal to maternal sentiment to pacify the mob, in vain, as we know, since the king and queen were taken prisoners and were later executed on the Place de la Concorde. In the palace are shown the bed-room and the private rooms of Louis XIV. The most enchanting sight here, though, are the magnificent gardens. In every direction there are beautifully laid off gardens, with lakes and fountains—too exquisite a scene for the pen to describe. The galleries of the palace contain valuable paintings of the French battles, of the French Kings and generals. The statue here of Napoleon, representing him during the last years at St. Helena, is very imposing, so forcefully are depicted the attitude and expression of the weary, disappointed despot. The portraits of Josephine are beautiful. The one of her when the Emperor makes known his intentions of marrying another and divorcing her is especially sad and appealing to those who know that regretful event of the general's life.

Coming back to the gay city, an interesting sight to me was the beautiful Iles des Chiens. So, not only is the Parisian women's love for her "dogie" evidenced on the car by affectionate caresses and kisses, but here in this cemetery by handsome statues and monuments.

But of all the beauties of the city of Paris, not excepting the grand operas, the many palaces, the lovely parks and gardens, the noted churches and cathedrals, not even the famous drive Champs Elysees and the Seine with its many bridges, I say, of all the beauties of Paris the most pleasant and the most enjoyable one to me was the fine equestrian statue of our own George Washington, which greeted me unexpectedly as I walked down the Seine to the Trocadero palace.

Alonzo Cleveland Hall.
Paris, July 20, 1908.

INGRAM, VA.

The last second Saturday was a splendid day at Ingram Church. It was Children's Day. Nature smiled in all her glory. The sky was clear and everything seemed serene and beautiful, charmed with nature's activities. Some said 800 people were there. The children had been carefully trained by the highly accomplished Miss Nannie Carlton, who had been so faithful in making possible the success of the day. The recitations were beautifully rendered and the music edifying. Bro. Ingle, of South Boston, gave an interesting address on "Character Building." A nice offering was given and a bountiful dinner spread before an appreciative audience. Thus passed into history a good day for Ingram, just such as could be expected by so noble-hearted people as constitute that splendid congregation.

S. B. Klapp.
Greensboro, N. C.

Keyser.

Bro. Wm. Keith was ordained a deacon in the Keyser church last third Sunday evening to fill the vacancy in the death of Bro. C. H. Van Dousen. Bro. Keith is one of our best Christians as well as one of the best business men in Keyser, and no doubt the church made a wise selection in him.

We are sorry to note the feeble condition of little Willie Keith, who is in Sanford hospital under an operation, though he is supposed to be doing very well.

S. B. Klapp.

Argo Red Salmon,—Try it.

THE SUNDAY SCHOOL.

Third Quarter, Lesson VII, Aug. 16, '08·
...... Saul Tries to Kill David... ....
Golden Text.—Jehovah God is a sun
and a shield. Psalm 84:11.

While Saul was king of Israel he had
many things to trouble him. One day
"Saul went to. Jesse, saying, let David,
I pray thee, stand before me, for he hath
found favor in my sight. And it came
to pass, when the evil spirit was upon
Saul, that David took an harp, and played with his hands. So Saul was refresh-
ed and was well, and the evil spirit departed from him."

David loved Saul, but Saul was jealous of David, and did not treat him well.
One time when David was returning
from a battle in which they had killed
a great many of their enemies, the wom-
en and children of Israel went out to
meet them and the women sang, "Saul
has slain his thousand and David his ten
thousands." Now Saul was very angry
when he heard the women giving David
so much praise, and he said, "What can·
he have more than the kingdom?" Saul
remembered what Samuel had told him,
and he was always watching David, for
Saul thought David would be the one
who would take the kingdom from him.
So the next day after the women sang
their praises of David, an evil spirit
came upon Saul. And Saul had a javelin in his hand, and he threw it at David
and said he would smite him to the wall.
Think you that God will turn away
and give to the enemy those who have
thrown themselves upon him for mercy
and protection? Nay, verily, He is their
shield and their exceeding great reward.

About this time of the year, those who
go into the country picnicking, are apt
have a sad experience if they touch a
certain plant that grows in the woods.
Every one dreads poison ivy. The poison gets into the blood and causes pain.
Poison makes one suffer and may cause
death.

When Saul threw his javelin at David,
it was because of the poison in his heart,
which paralyzed his affections and spoiled his happiness.

How do doctors cure a poisoned person? By an antidote. What is the antidote for envy and jealousy? Loving interest in others. It is thinking too much
about self that makes a person suffer
from envy. Two things we can do to
keep envy from poisoning our lives. To
be in earnest to do our best, and a genuine love for others.

From F. K. Sanders, in S. S. Times.

The story of the life of David is full
of puzzles to the historian who reads
closely, but all versions agree in the data
on which we lay most stress,—the at-

tractive personality of David, his splendid exhibition of faith and prowess, the
extravagant adulation of the people over his. deeds, his immediate success as
an officer, the sudden jealousy of Saul,
and the means taken by that sovereign
to get rid of him.

No more telling indication of Saul's
lack of balance could be given than his
foolish hatred of David. The young
man rejoiced over his place at court, was
truly loyal to Saul, his patron, conceived
a deep affection for Jonathan, Saul's
son, and was quite incapable of the
treachery which Saul supposed he had
discovered. In David Saul had a servant who could have strengthened his
hold. upon the people of his kingdom.
Instead, he. forced him to become an op-
ponent· and the leader of ·an opposition.

There is a charm in the enthusiasm
of David at this time.. He is willing to
dare any deed for the sake of the re-
wards he values, and when he saw the
lion and the bear making havoc with the
sheep confided to his care, or as when he
heard the vaunting challenge of the gi-
gantic Philistine, his personal danger in an outburst of
genuine indignation, and rose to the need
of the moment. When the king gave him
a post of peril in his army his bravery
but added to the luster of his name.
When by reason of Michal's affection
for David, Saul demanded of him a proof
of prowess which would make him a
marked foe of the dangerous Philistines,
David rendered double service.

All these successes on David's part
had the effect of widening the breach between Saul and the one who had become
his foremost subject. The king, so perfect physically, so lovable in many ways,
was consumed with jealous rage. Thus
was showwn the fatal defect in character which neutralized his unquestioned
ability. His jealousy bred suspicion,
and this led to such meanness and mal-
ice and bitter hatred that his inability
to govern himself, least of all a nation
as its king, was made only too striking-
ly evident to all. Saul's pursuit of
David was a continuous exhibition of his
degeneracy. With every measure taken
to drive the beloved young leader from
his presence and to take his life, Saul re-
ally added to David's hold upon the
people and to his own confusion. The
people loved David more and more, and
set their minds upon him as a hero and
friend and leader.

Jealousy is a disease, like leprosy. It
deadens the soul, makes it unresponsive
to the dictates of judgment or holiness.
Jealousy rarely, if ever, is of positive
value. It grows out of selfishness and
excessive pride. It always belittles and
weakens both parties.

Lesson Teachings.

1. It is easier to cheer after battle
than to encourage before.

2. Jealousy assigns evil intentions to
the innocent.

3. Popularity brings dangers in its
wake.   G. W. Tickle.

ELON COLLEGE NOTES.

President Moffitt has been spending
the past week at Elon College attending
to office correspondence and preparing
for the next session. He is very much
encouraged by the reports from the
field. He has prosecuted a vigorous
campaign · and reports from canvassers
indicate an increase of new students.
Much work has been done in new territory, especially in Eastern N. C. and
South Carolina. The president's correspondence is unusually heavy.

In the number of canvassers and the
territory visited this summer breaks all
previous records. Our men have done
six weeks of hard faithful work· and
deserve a well earned rest for two
weeks before opening of the session. Mr.
Pritchette has spent some time in S. C.
and Mr. J. A. Vaughn and Mr. A. L. Lincoln in Eastern North Carolina in the interest of the college.

Mrs. C. E. Newman, of Henderson,
N. C., principals H. M. Loy, of Jackson Graded Schools, W. M. Brown, of
Lexington Graded Schools, A. L. Lincoln, of Haw River Graded School, De
Roy Fonville, law student, University
of Va., Chamness Davidson, of Fayette-
ville Graded Schools, Miss Effie Iseley,
of Chipley High School, Ga., have visited their alma mater recently. One of
Elon's largest assets is the devotion of
her alumni.

Mr. Chamness Davidson is in the St.
Leo Hospital for appendicitis.

Miss Iola Kernodle was elected assist-
ant last fall in Roanoke Island Graded
School. So pleased were the patrons
that at Christmas she was chosen principal. As announced in the Sun, she
has recently married.

Miss Lenora Franks teaches in the
Burlington Graded School next session.
Miss Ella Brunk teaches in New Mex-
ico.

Dolph Long is studying in Summer
Law School, State University.

S. E. Denton has been reelected principal of Clayton, Ala., Schools. He has
been at the University of Ala. standing
examination for his M. A.

D. J. Sipe has located in Greensboro
and is taking an active interest in our
Greensboro work. Is Sec'y of the C. E.

Prof. Lincoln is principal of Williams
ton Graded School.   E. C.

RELIGION FIRST.

"Seek ye first the kingdom of God and his righteousness, and all these things shall be added unto you."—Matt. 6:33.

Our text suggests two propositions:

That the Kingdom of God and his righteousness are so related to our earthly necessities that, if we seek the former, we shall also receive the latter.

That we should seek the Kingdom of God and His righteousness first.

Let us consider the relation of the Kingdom of God and His righteousness to the things necessary to this life.

The Kingdom of God, as our Savior speaks of it in the text, is God's rule over those who will accept it, here in this life. There is, of course, a heavenly kingdom also; but Christ's exhortation is that we seek the Kingdom now, while eating and drinking and wearing clothes are necessary. The Kingdom and righteousness, then, is not "other-worldliness," but right relations to God and man in this world, loyalty and obedience to God, righteousness toward man, very much what we sum up in the word "religion."

Now, is it not altogether likely that one who cordially accepts the rule of God in God's own world, and seeks to be in right relation with God and man, should receive the things essential to life, such as food and raiment? Or is it at all likely that God would have established a kingdom among men which would make no provision for the needs of the body? Is it likely that he would consider a course in life right, or righteous, which did not include these necessary things? Would any just ruler do so?

As sovereign of the Kingdom, God would naturally supply to His faithful subjects, if they themselves could not secure them, these needful things. Is it possible that "our Father" would want His children to be hungry and thirsty and shabby? that the God of wisdom, love, and power would not know how, and be willing and able to provide these things?

Furthermore, the laws of the Kingdom tend toward the supply of our bodily needs. The main law governing the relation of the subjects of the Kingdom is, "Thou shalt love thy neighbor as thyself." Now it is inconceivable that we should live up to this law, and not do enough for our neighbors, to earn a living.

Many of the minor laws of the Kingdom tend toward worldly prosperity. such is the law, "Six days shalt thou labor and do all thy work," or the exhortation to be, "not slothful in business, fervent in spirit, serving the Lord." or, "Be temperate in all things." It is hardly conceivable that we should observe these laws of the Kingdom and not have all necessary things added unto us.

Observation proves that the citizens of the Kingdom are rarely destitute of "these things." The Psalmist was doubtless a man of wide experience; and he says, "I have been young and now am old; yet have I not seen the righteous forsaken, nor his seed begging bread." Such is a very general experience. Nearly every Christian who has lived long and observed widely, can say the same. Paul, who had done both, tells Timothy in a confidential letter that "Godliness is profitable unto all things, having promise of the life that now is and of that which is to come." Dr. Crafts tells us that 75 per cent of the leading merchants of Chicago are professed Christians. That is to say, they observe the laws of the Kingdom, outwardly at least.

To say, as some have, that it takes something more than the Kingdom of Heaven and its righteousness to get along in this world is to misapprehend the scope of the Kingdom. As has been said already, it is not "other-worldliness," a matter of beliefs and feelings and hopes. It is living in this world as the Creator of the world would have us live; its righteousness is the condition of being in right relations with everything in this world.

We should seek the Kingdom of Heaven and His righteousness first. We have already learned the reason for doing so: "All these things shall be added." We are sure not to make a failure of this life if we do so. If, however, we thrust the Kingdom and righteousness into the second place, and seek first the things of this world, we may, or may not, secure the things of this world, but we can not get into the Kingdom or attain to its righteousness in that way. We can not serve God and mammon.

But there is a vastly higher reason. It is God's Kingdom. Surely we would not think of thrusting His claims into a lower place than first! It is a question of righteousness, of being as far as in us lies in right relation with God and man. Shall we make that secondary? A great statesman, thinking of the loftiest earthly prize possible to a statesman, said, "I would rather be right than be President." That is, desirable as he deemed it to fill the loftiest station on earth, he sought righteousness first. Shall we then first seek what we shall eat, or what we shall drink, or wherewithal we shall be clothed, and then, if time serves, seek to know and obey the will of God, and enter into right relations with all mankind? Shall we keep the King of kings waiting our decision while we eat and drink and dress? No, first

"Trust in God, and do the right,"

and then there will be ample time to get all these things. Indeed you will not have to seek them; for if you seek the Kingdom, you will find them also.

What then does it imply that we seek the Kingdom and its righteousness first? Surely, whatever else it implies, it means that we seek it first in order of time, that we begin the search before we eat a meal or dress for another day; that we begin it now.—Rev. David Keppel, New York, in Homiletic Review.

THE WOMAN WHO MAKES GOOD.
She Possesses Many Things, but Most of All Common Sense.

The woman who makes good must be blessed with strength and health and an ambition to learn and take advantage of every opportunity that comes her way, says the September Delineator.

She must work with all her heart; play with all her heart; above all things avoiding indifference and the enemy to all progress—apathy.

She must select the pleasure that will bring her the greatest joy, choose the work she is best fitted for.

Ordinary hard luck never ruins people. It puts them in a mood to learn a thing or two. Everybody makes mistakes. With some it is a regular occupation; but to make a mistake and wail about it is to make two.

Women often speak of their talents not being appreciated. A talent is next to worthless unless one has the ability to get down to hard, plain, every-day grind.

Then, too, the woman who wins must learn to talk, but not to tell. There is an art—the most consummate art—in appearing absolutely frank to the butcher, the baker, and the family cat and yet not reveal any of one's business affairs. The woman who wins must be able to hold all and hear all yet betray it by neither word nor look; by injudicious defense no more than by overt treachery; by anger at a malicious accusation no more than by a smile at an egregious mistake. To be able to do this requires a rare combination of tact and self-respect. One cannot slide along in business and win promotion and more salary. A knowledge of the business is necessary to show results.

To make good, a woman needs that fine balance, that accurate self-measurement, which goes by the name of common sense. It is the one thing on which success depends the most.

THE CHRISTIAN SUN.

Founded 1844 by Elder Daniel W. Kerr.
Organ of the Southern Christian
Convention.

Entered at the postoffice at Greensboro, N. C., as second-class matter.

Terms of Subscription.

One Year $1.50
Six Months .... .75
Four Months .... .50
Advertising rates given on application.

J. O. Atkinson, Editor and Publisher.

Important Notice.—As readers will
see, The Christian Sun is now published
at Greensboro, N. C. The office of publication there is 302½ South Elm Street.
Our editorial office, however, remains at
Elon College, N. C., to which all letters
and communications to the Editor should
be addressed, as heretofore.

CHURCH WORK.

It is not difficult to secure, or induce,
workers for the church. Most are willing. More often the opportunity is lacking. What most churches need is to
give its members an opportunity. There
are thousands of good members, intelli-
gent and worthy, who have never been
asked, or given the privilege, to under-
take anything in the name and for the
sake of the church.

"There isn't a member in our church
who can, or will, lead in public prayer,
be superintendent of the Sunday school,
or take the lead in any service," said a
complainant recently. We doubt if the
list had been exhausted, and we are certain that every member had not tried
and failed.

How is it known that no member of
the church or school can act as superintendent, other than the one now serving?
Have any others been tried? Have others been selected and put into the place?
Observation shows that most are mod-
est in such undertaking, and few indeed will seek position and work in the
church. But when sought, importuned,
petitioned, advised, men and women are
reluctant to say, No, as touching work
for the church.

Not of the public places only. There
are other places of work. Have you
known members to decline a task laid
upon them for the church? Not often.
Were they asked to solicit funds, fix up
the church yard, get some flowers for
the pulpit, help to keep the building in
order, take care of the hymn books, or
run errands for the church or Sunday
school? And did they refuse? Not oft-
en.

One reason, and a very great one, why
we have so few "church workers," is
because we call upon so few to work in,
about, or for the church.

And nothing is needed more. That for
which one gives of time, attention, and
thought, wins the heart, and holds the
interest and deep concern.

CHRISTIANITY PRACTICAL.

In recent issues of the Sun it has been
maintained that Christianity is not a
dream, or even a theoretical or impracticable scheme. That which touches, or
should touch, every phase of a man's
daily life, we have repeated, is not to
be called theoretical or impractical.
When the divine decree went forth, to
love one's neighbor as oneself, it was
based on the eternal fact that such a
manner and mode of love and living was
not only possible but practicable. Moreover, it was for the best to all mankind,
that men act in that fashion.

Or farber. "Seek ye first the kingdom of God and his righteousness and
all these things shall be added." That
was not given as theory. It was given
as the solidest and sanest fact of the
best experienced and most successful living. The impossible becomes possible
and the impractical becomes practical,
through the grace and power of God in
man. That which is theory with man
is deepest fact and most abiding reality
with God. Along this line we were
pleased to see in the New York Observer
a most weighty word to this end:

What is it that our Lord demands of
us? This first, that we value the life
more than the meat, the riches of the
spirit above the beauty of the garment.
Whether this mount of vision be attain-
able or not we will submit for judgment not to the invalid, but to the ath-
lete, no lover of pleasure, but to lov-
ers of God. Every year sees mountain
peaks hitherto regarded inaccessible
scaled. Every year Christian life rises
to a diviner ether and an ampler air.
Even in an age known for its devotion to
material ends the Church has its tens
of thousands of sons to whom duty is
not a hard task, but the voice of God
and heaven, not some far off event, but
a present possession.

And when our Lord adds to this the
demand that we "Seek first the kingdom
of God and his righteosness," surely no
one but the father of lies would declare
"impractical" what is wrought every
day. The business man whose first question is not, "Will it pay?" but "Is it
right?" is not a hero of romance. We
meet him every hour in the busiest places of the market. He is in the pulpit,
living upon $1,000 a year although offer-
ed twice that much in trade. He is in

wildest Africa teaching the Sermon on
the Mount to the children of cannibals,
while he might have read the Gospels
from an art lectern or preached about
heaven from a marble pulpit on the ave-
nue.

"Thou shalt love thy neighbor as thyself." "Impossible!" Why impossible
when men are doing it every day? The
workman who puts aside his own claim,
founded upon good work and long service, that a shop-mate with sick wife and
dependent children may be promoted,
loves his fellow better than his own interest. Whoever, conscious of strength
and vigor, steps aside that the weak and
the lame in life be not turned out of the
way but helped to reach his goal, is doing just what the Master demands. In
an age when Chile and Argentine sell
their battle-ships and erect a statue of
Christ upon the mountain top which con-
stitutes their boundary line, it is no time
to declare impractical that golden rule
which our late honored secretary of
state declared the sum and substance of
all modern international law.

It is the impossible that gives life all
its value. While the many scoffed, the
"impractical" theorists went on and
completed their impossible railways, and
impracticable ocean cables, and absurd
dynamos, and ridiculous wireless tele-
graphs, and so comes in the modern
world. And so will come that kingdom
of heaven wherein righteousness will
dwell just because there have always
been men to believe that things impracticable to man's unaided strength are
possible through him with whom all
things worth doing at all are forever
possible.

The editor received message Monday
morning that his daughter, Mary D.,
was worse of typhoid fever, and he left
for Norfolk at once.

Rev. J. W. Holt assisted Pastor C. C.
Peel in a gracious revival at Hines
Chapel, Guilford County, last week.
There were four confessions, four addi-
tions, four baptisms, the church much
revived.

Rev. L. E. Smith is spending a busy
vacation, having averaged preaching
once per day every day since commence-
ment. Much of his time has been spent
among home churches of the Alabama
Conference. The past week he has conducted a successful revival at Ramseur,
N. C., there being three additions to the
church. At O'Kelly's, another of Bro.
Smith's churches, there were five conversions. He is this and next week assisting Pastor L. I. Cox in Rockingham
County. Bro. Smith will re-enter Elon
College at the opening in September.

ELON COLLEGE.

A Fine Opening in Prospect.

This will be the last week for the active canvass for students for Elon for the year 1908-09; and, as I look back over the work that has been done and the reports that have been made by the professors who have been in the canvass, I feel that the college and the church are indeed fortunate in haveing such men to labor in their behalf. With that faithfulness and zeal that have ever characterized them in all their endeavors, they have vigorously presented the claims of the college in many sections of North Carolina, Virginia, and South Carolina, during the past five weeks; and, as a result we are looking forward to the best opening in the histoory of the College. The second day of September will be a bright, glad day at Elon, and all will receive a cordial welcome.

The indications are that a larger percentage of the old students will return than heretofore, and the number of new students promised is unusually large. It will be very helpful, however, if our old students and other friends in the various sections will continue to encourage the young people who have "promised," or who are "prospective," to hold steadfast to their purpose to get an education and to get it at Elon College. It oftentimes requires an effort on the part of a young boy or girl to leave home and go away to school for the first time. They need not only the canvassing of the teacher, but the encouraging and hopeful prospect that their friends may hold out before them. Many boys and girls miss an education because of a lack of courage to break away from home surroundings, and to take up what seems to them to be the "hard life" of the student. They need those who "have been there" to tell them that it is not a hard life at all, but that it is a life full of the highest type of pleasure as well as of profit to those who covet the best gifts. Ask any college man or woman what has been the most pleasant and helpful period of his career, and in almost every instance he will tell you that it was his college life. There is something about it that not only strengthens the mind, but at the same time lightens the heart, and makes us feel that life is all the more worth living.

To Our Patrons.

We would like to urge upon parents the importance of having their sons and daughters here at the opening. Every student ought to be in place the very first day, September 2, and begin at the beginning. It means more to him than oftentimes he or his parents think, to begin with the first exercise—it gives him an even chance with his fellow-student, and relieves him of embarrassment, and at the same time of the unpleasant and unsatisfactory task of "catching up."

Annual Reception.

Students will note that the opening reception this year is the first Friday evening, Sept. 4th, instead of the second, as heretofore. This is always one of the most pleasant events of the year, for both old and new students, and it is hoped that this year it may be even more pleasant, if possible, than in former years.

Club Board.

Arrangements are being made for one, and possibly two, boarding clubs for young men where those who wish to do so may get their board at first cost. These clubs will be under excellent management, and will be able to provide for all those who may wish to take their meals with them.

Let every friend of Elon who has an opportunity, speak a word for the college during the next three weeks, and help to turn a student Elon-ward. Some of the best canvassing is done by our friends, especially our old students. We are to have a student this year from Memphis, Tenn., thanks to the good word and works of an old Elon "boy" —our friend, Rev. B. F. Black, who is Secretary of the Street Ry. Y. M. C. A. in Memphis, and in the same way many others help year after year to build up our college, and at the same time to lead their friends into broader spheres of usefulness in life.

In behalf of the professors who have done the canvassing, and also of the College, I wish to express our appreciation of the many kindnesses that have been shown us during the summer, in our work. Without such generous assistance, we could not have expected such a promising outlook for the coming year's work.

E. L. Moffitt, Pres.

TEACHER TRAINING—WHY?

In this age of specialists and specialism, of wide research and accurate knowledge, it is almost superfluous to ask why we should train ourselves for any undertaking. We have trained acrobats and athletes, trained wood-choppers and water-drawers, trained musicians and singers, trained this and trained the other, everything must be especially prepared for, from the making of pins to the launching of ocean-goers, and everybody must be specially prepared, except, I had almost said, Sunday school teachers. We insist on our secular teachers being specially prepared. We would not send to a public school, the teacher of which could not pass the county examination. And yet a great many of us never think that special training is also an essential to success in good Sunday school teaching. Behold our consistency!

Yes, this age demands preparation, training, for every department of its intricate, complex organization. No man who is a Jack-at-all-trades is needed in the world's work today. It is the man with one eye and with that centered on one thing that succeeds in our era of rigid standards and yet more rigid competition. And it is getting to be more so every day. The time when men rise to greatness and to fame without special training has passed. The man with trained head, trained hand, and trained heart, he is the man that the world looks to for doing its work and him it will crown with success.

Sunday school teachers are no exception to the rule. We Sunday school teachers are human, like the secular teachers. We have something of the divine in the message we present and in the high prerogatives of the office we exercise, but we are ourselves no more divine than other people—we are just plain, ordinary, human flesh and blood, brawn and brain, and we must take account of our powers and the laws of their development and fruition just as our fellowmen do. If they must prepare for their secular functions, we must prepare for our sacred ones, and unless we do, we may expect to be only second-rate teachers, poor expounders of the word of life, sorry representatives of Him of whom it was said, "Never man spake as He spake." To be specially and thoroughly trained is to teach with authority—to teach with authority is to teach successfully and with power.

We Sunday school teachers need to prepare for our great work, to train ourselves for our holy function, that we may be successful teachers, fit leaders of those committed to our care, good shepherds of the flocks of Israel, worthy citizens of the commonwealth of God. Ours is the noblest work in the world—we are what our Master was—teachers. Let us be as careful in our preparation as we can be, to the end that, like Him, we may teach with authority and so with success.

W. A. Harper, Chairman
Committee on Teacher
Training.

Berea Christian Church, Alamance Co., N. C., will be dedicated fifth Sunday in August. The pastor, Rev. C. C. Peel, extends a cordial invitation to the brethren, especially pastors, to be present.

CHILDREN'S CORNER.

The Band of Cousins.

Jas. L. Foster, Sec., Elon College, N. C.

"He that hath pity on the poor lendeth unto the Lord, and his good deed will He pay him again."—Prov. 19:17.

Total reported last week......$998.84

Dues.

Baird Moffitt	.30
J. Newman Denton	.10
S. E. Denton, Jr.	.10
John Hill	.10

Monthly S. S. Offering.

Union Grove, Kemp's Mills, N. C.	1.00
Linville, Va.	3.70
Hayes Chapel, N. C.	1.00
Henderson, N. C.	2.63
Antioch, Va.	2.13
Salem Chapel, N. C.	.66

Special Offering.

Mrs. Lucy J. Barker	.25
Amount 29th week,	—— $1010.81

My Dear Children:

Our family is not quite so large this week as four of the children are visiting relatives. Mary and Everton Morris and Frances and Jack Kissell have gone to Sanford for a while. Miss Dora is taking a little vacation also, so we miss them very much. It makes quite a difference to have five out of a family at one time. Well, we have made some nice jelly out of two bushels of apples given by Mr. J. W. Sharp of Elon College and the girls and Mrs. Kissell are giving rooms, windows, etc., a good cleaning with some "Star Bright" polish, a can of which was given us by Mrs. L. M. Clymer of Greensboro, N. C. last week.

Our sick boys are entirely well now wanting to eat like little pigs. The health of the other children is splendid and the watermelons that are brought up by the wagon-load disappear as fast as we let the hungry boys and girls get hold of them. Misses Bessie and Myrtle King from Raleigh are now making us a visit and little Mary Lee and James are delighted.   Very cordially,   Uncle Jim.

Save the Machine

Put new life into the hard-worked sewing machine. Make it run lightly, noiselessly. Liven it and the hundred other things about the house that are getting "the worse for wear" with a little

Household Lubricant

Best of all oils for domestic purposes. Try it on the lawn mower, freezer, washer, bicycle, anything that needs oil. Won't corrode, gum, clog or tarnish.

Sold in handy-size, 4 and 8 ounce tin oilers. All dealers.

STANDARD OIL COMPANY
(INCORPORATED)

Asheboro N. C., July 28, 1908.
Dear Uncle Jim:—

It has been a long time since I wrote you, but I have not forgotten you and the cousins. When I was over at Elm in the spring mother took me to the Orphanage to see the little children. I enjoyed playing with them but was sorry I did not see you too. Since summer has come I have been having such a nice time and been so busy at play with my little cousins who have been visiting me. One of my aunties from Va. is coming tonight to stay a while with us. She is going to bring one of her little girls, so I am expecting a fine time playing croquet etc.

Do the little children at the orphanage ever catch rabbits for pets? I had one once but it got out and ran away. I did not care much, for I hated to see the poor little thing caged.

Fearing I will be too lengthy if I write more I will say good-night. Enclosed find my dues for the months I have failed to write.

Your little nephew,
Baird Moffitt.

We have missed your letters, Baird, and so glad to hear from you again. Hope you'll have a fine time with your cousin.

Sanford, N. C., Aug. 1, 1908.
Dear Uncle Jim:—

Had bad luck with my first offering, but I hope this time it will arrive safe. I have a little cousin Pauline, who says she is going to write to the corner. I like to play with her and get my hands tangled up in her hair, but don't think she likes it as well as I do. I'm just a wee man of seven months. You will hear from me again in a few weeks. With love to everyone of the little girls and boys in the Home.

John Hill.

Your money secure this time, John. Tell Pauline to be sure to write.

White Springs, Fla., July 20, 1908.
Dear Uncle Jim:—

We are off on a visit to friends and drinking sulphur water, too. We certainly enjoy seeing people bathe in the spring. This is such a pretty place—all the boys and girls would enjoy being here.

We send our love and dimes.
Fondly,
J. Newman Denton,
S. E. Denton, Jr.

Yes, indeed, you are fortunate, boys, to be enjoying a visit at the Springs.

STILL RUNNING.

Edwin, aged four, owned a picture book, in which a fierce-looking cow was running after a small boy. He looked at it a long time, then carefully closing the book he laid it away. A few days later he got the book again, and turned to the picture. Bringing his chubby fist down on the cow, he exclaimed in a tone of triumph, "She ain't caught him yet!"—The September Delineator.

DONALD KNEW.

Margaret, aged ten, was a beginner in history. "Mama," she asked, "what does 'behead' mean?"

"To cut off a man's head, dear."

There was a moment of silent study; then another question.

"What does 'defeat' mean, mama?"

Little Donald, aged four, was interested.

"I know, mama," was his logical conclusion. " 'Defeat' means to cut a man's feet off."—The September Delineator.

We love Him because He first loved us.—John.

NEWPORT NEWS LETTER.

When a curious crowd, including critical Scribes and Pharisees had witnessed the healing of a paralytic by Christ, they said, "We have seen strange things this day." To the idle looker-on there were many strange things on that particular day. The healing of the paralytic, Christ reading the unexpressed thoughts of the Pharisees, were all strange to them. Then in Christ's day, there were many strange things, in the natural heart renewed by grace, the creator born an infant, death slain by the dying of a man. But in our day there are, if possible, stranger things. It is strange that man should be daring and blind to his own good as to take his eternal interest in his own hands, and in the face of light and truth turn his back on the only hope in the universe for him. Strange that he should close his eyes to the light, and refuse to believe the most rational and real thing in the world while accepting other things on less evidence, and which are of less importance. It is strange that some professing to be filled with the spirit of Christ, to be walking in his footsteps, and to be his representatives, should be so filled, like the Scribes and Pharisees, with criticism and censure for those of the fold who in in weakness, or by misguided judgement, have made mistakes. The Word exhorts that, "If any man be overtaken in a fault ye which are spiritual restore such a one in the spirit of meekness" And again that marvellous lesson on love declares, "Love thinketh no evil." And still again, "Bear ye one another's burdens and so fulfill the law of Christ."

We found a man who by misguided judgment had innocently made a blunder. In it he felt keenly afflicted and distressed. Quickly following that, there came to his life a misfortune in way of a providence for which he was in no way responsible. It placed him where he could easily be misinterpreted and misjudged, and where uncomplimentary things might be said of him with some indication to the public mind that they might be true. His only hope in his distress was that the love of God and sympathy of his brethren, with the grace of God, would enable him to endure and survive. Instead, however, while God's grace sustained, his brethren were critical and heaped censure upon him while his heart and life were burdened almost beyond endurance already. The worst was that instead of going to him with loving counsel, and offering to him their censure in a brotherly way, he found that among themselves they were discussing and criticing his life and conduct, and advertising even in remote places what seemed to be true of him but which in reality was unreal and untrue. We found him once at the point of desperation, and by earnest encouragement and counsel, with the help of a few others, his broken spirits were revived and yet for the lack of that which it was the duty of his brethren to extend his usefulness was hindered, his spirit broken, and his life spoiled. Shall we wait for the funeral to scatter roses? It is not only our privilege but our duty as Christians to "scatter seeds of kindness" along the pathway of those with whom we travel here. To cheer a drooping spirit, encourage a brother or sister in an hour of despondency, is indeed a privilege. I have found but one class for whom Christ had censure and that was the hypocrite. To the backslider and poor fellow possessed of devils, and sinful woman, He expressed nothing but love and pity. We are Christian only in so far as we express the Christ spirit. "I live, yet not I but Christ liveth in me; and the life which I now live in the flesh I live by the faith of the Son of God." It might be a helpful exercise to often ask, "Am I my brother's keeper?"

Murdock W. Butler.

DISTRICT MEETING PROGRAM.

District meeting at Flint Hill Christian Church, Clay, Co., Alabama, embracing fifth Sunday in August.

Friday, Aug. 28, 7:30 P. M.
Preaching by Rev. B. H. Veazey.

Saturday, Aug. 29, 9 A. M.
Meeting called to order by President. Enrollment of Ministers and delegates. Election of officers.

9:30 A. M.—Subject, What Has Been Accomplished by the District Meeting? Rev. C. M. Dollar.

10 A. M.—What Is Expected of Me as a Member of the Church of Christ, J. C. Knight and J. J. Carter.

10:30 A. M.—The Relation of the Pastor to His People, Rev. J. H. Hughes.

The Relation of the People to Their Pastor, Welker Pearson.

11 A. M.—Sermon by Rev. E. M. Carter.

Refreshments.

1:30 P. M.—What Is the Best Method of Raising Money With Which to Build Church Houses, E. M. Gay and J. H. Milam.

2 P. M.—Is Money Thus Expended a Gift, or Is It an Investment by the Individual? R. A. Gay, and C. M. Dollar.

2:30 P. M.—What Can We Do to Extend the Borders of the Alabama Conference? G. O. Lankford and W. E. Pate.

3 P. M.—Why Do We Believe in Missions Home and Foreign? E. M. Carter and J. D. Dollar.

CANCER CAN BE CURED.

My Mild Combination Treatment is used by the patient at home. Years of success. Hundreds of testimonials. Endorsed by physicians, ministers, etc. The local application destroys Cancerous growth, and the constitutional treatment eliminates the disease from the system, preventing its return. Write for Free Book, "Cancer and its Cure." No matter how serious your case, no matter how many operations you have had, no matter what treatment you have tried, do not give up hope but write at once. Dr. Johnson Remedy Co., 1235 Grand Ave., Kansas City, Mo.

MEDICINE.

We prepare as good medicine, the very best medicine that the finest, freshest, most potent drugs and chemicals will produce when carefully and skilfully compounded by an expert prescription man—just such medicine as your physician means that you should have, medicine of the utmost possible effectiveness. May we prepare your medicine?

FREEMAN DRUG CO.,
Burlington, N. C.

King's Business College
(INCORPORATED)

Capital Stock, $30,000.00 Business. When you think of going off to school, write for new Catalogue Journal and Special Offers of the leading Business and Shorthand Schools. Address King's Business College, Raleigh, N. C., or Charlotte, N. C. (We also teach Book-keeping, Short-hand, Penmanship, etc., by mail.)

To Drive Out Malaria and Build up the System.

Take the Old Standard GROVE'S TASTELESS CHILL TONIC. You know what you are taking. The formula is plainly printed on every bottle, showing it is simply Quinine and Iron in a tasteless form, and the most effectual form. For grown people and children. 50c.

3:30 P. M.—Query Box, conducted by the president.

Miscellaneous Business.

7:30 P. M.—Preaching by G. O. Lankford.

Sunday, 9 A. M.
Prayer service.

9:30 A. M.—Why Should Each Church or Community Have a Sunday School?

10 A. M.—Things Most Needful to the Church Spiritually. Opened, by E. M. Carter.

11 A. M.—Preaching by Rev. C. M. Dollar, The Principles of the Christian Church, followed by the Communion service.

C. W. Carter,
G. D. Hunt,
G. W. Evans,
Committee.

SUNDAY SCHOOL HOME MISSIONS.

(An Address before the N. C. and Va. Sunday School Convention, by Rev. J. W. Holt.)

Ever since our Savior said to his disciples, "Go ye therefore and teach all nations" (Matt. 28:17) the great work of the church has been recognized as Missions. Aggressive tactics are essential to success in the conquest of all alien territory. Darkness recedes before approaching light, and relinquishes its hold many times upon priceless possessions. The church is now the light of the world and God's ally in the work of the world's salvation. It has long been admitted that teaching the children divine truth is a duty that the church owes to itself and to the world. Its future success and growth depends upon the fidelity with which this duty is met.

1st. What shall the church do? All things that the Master enjoined as necessary to glorify Him and to advance His kingdom. The farmer teaches his son to till the soil and plant seed and cultivate the crop that the harvest may be satisfactory. Nearly every farmer's son wants to have his own patch of wheat, corn, melons, he wants his own horse, wagon, axe, and gun. Whatever he sees his father do he tries to do. By this procedure agriculture is promoted in the nation: The son is but the juvenile farmer. The juvenile farmer is not an ally of the farmer but an adjunct to the farm—an indispensible accompaniment to the perpetuity and progress of agriculture. Every principle involved and every argument applied in the case of the farmer and his son may be adduced in the case of the mother and her daughter, the merchant and his sons, the teacher and his children, the church and the Sunday school. It is not merely an alliance, but a mutual cooperation that should be recognized between them. If the church works in the field of missions the Sunday school may very properly enter the same ground. It should be allowed to inaugurate and to prosecute its own special efforts to establish and spread the Gospel. No man would think of holding tenaciously to the truth in his conversation with others without caring whether his son adhered to the truth or not. Rather he would feel much mortified to know that his son paid no regard to the truth. Every industrious father loves to see industrious habits observed by son, even when quite young, What then should the church teach? Just what the Master taught. The Sunday school of today will be largely the church of tomorrow. Would we have a mission church filled with the mission spirit, then that spirit must be

inculcated in our Sunday schools. This can be successfully done only by giving the Sunday school something to do in the field of missions. It may be only a small beginning at first, but good seed will produce good crops if planted in good soil and well-cultivated. Youthful hearts and minds are fertile ground in which to plant the seeds of Christian liberality, and youthful hands are susceptible of great activity in the service of the Master. The last session of the North Carolina and Virginia Christian Conference adopted a suggestion of the Committee on Home Missions. This is the first suggestion to our schools to enter this field directly and inaugurate a special work to be prosecuted as Sunday school Home Missions. It is hoped that many of our schools will take hold of this work.

Lanett, Alabama.

I have charge of the following churches; Lanett, Lagrange, Langdale, and Riverview. also an appointment at a new point between Langdale and Riverview. We expect to organize a church at this place soon. This is a mill town of about 2,000 population, and we expect to enter at once and go to work for the Lord. My appointment is at Lagrange on the 1st Sunday, The Lord has done a great work there this year. We held our revival at this place beginning July 1 and continuing ten days. Bro. L, E. Smith was with us then and a gracious outpouring of the Holy Spirit. There were

thirty-eight additions to the church; twenty-eight were baptised. From there we went to Langdale and held ten days' meeting at this place. Bro. L. E. Smith did the preaching and the power of the Holy Spirit was felt from beginning to end. Eleven were added to the church. Bro. T. H. Elder was with us at this place. Bro. Tom. while old, is still giving his service to the cause of the church and the kingdom.

We have not held our meeting at Lanett and Riverview yet. While we have not held the protracted meeting at these places I have received into the church at Lanett fifteen members; Riverview, five. I am just back home from Brown's Spring Church where Bro. West and myself held 7 days and the power of God was manifested. The pastor, Bro. Willington, had to leave the day following the day I arrived. We received 24 into the church at this place. We left this church revived and in good working condition, On Monday following the 4th Sunday in March I visited a town called Millsteat 30 miles north east of Atlanta and held a two weeks' meeting. The Lord blessed us in this meeting: The week following the fourth Sunday in May I visited this place again and held a week's meeting. These meetings were the first of our denomination in this place. During two months there were fifty members who joined the M. E. and Baptist churches, and if we had had a church there we would have gotten a part of them. They are giving the Macedonian cry, come over and help us. Brethren, what are we to do? My time is all filled and I have promised to go back and help them some time this fall and will leave it with the conference whether we will organize there or not.

Brethren, pray over this work. My work this year has been crowned with success. I have received into my churches this year 73 members for which I give God the praise. My next work will be the first week, with Bro. G. O. Langford at Pleasant Grove; the week following with Bro. J. M. Milem at Rock Spring Church. Pray for us that the Holy Spirit may be with us. My salary has been paid very well so far and my conference claims are a little behind but will come up alright. Brethren, I trust we shall have the best report this year we have ever had. Pray for me that I may do my whole duty in the work; that I may live a Christian life and be more useful in the Lord's hands.

B. F. Young.

20,000 TELEGRAPH OPERATORS NEEDED.—YOUNG MEN, PREPARE YOURSELVES FOR GOOD POSITIONS.

On account of the new 8-hour law passed by Congress in the interest of telegraphers, and also on account of so many new railroads being built and old lines extended, an unusual demand for operators has been created. Conservative estimates have placed the number of additional operators that will be required during the next ten months at approximately 20,000.

YOUNG MEN, NOW IS YOUR OPPORTUNITY! Enroll in our school NOW and in only four to six months we will have you qualified for splendid positions. Telegraph operators receive from $50.00 upwards. Our school has been established twenty years; its equipment is perfect; instruction thorough and practical; positions positively guaranteed our graduates. Board in Newnan is very cheap; the town is healthful and the people are cordial. Two Main Line Railroad Wires run into our school rooms. No other school in the United States has such up-to-date and practical facilities for the benefit of its students. Write at once for free descriptive literature.

Southern School of Telegraphy, Newnan, Georgia.

TIRED BRAIN

means that you are losing control of your will power; it is difficult to concentrate your thoughts; you are forgetful, languid, nervous, irritable. Refresh your tired brain with Dr. Miles' Nervine, which will soothe, feed and strengthen the exhausted nerves, and renew your brain power. The first bottle will not fail to help you; if so, your druggist will return your money.

Argo Red Salmon is caught in Bering Sea among the icebergs. That is why the fish is so firm and the flavor so delicious.

TEN WAYS OF PRAYING.

1. The formal way—when prayer is a mere form of words, with little or no heart; or when it is simply due to the force of habit which has lost its real motive power.

2. The hurried way—hastening through it as a disagreeable and irksome duty—a duty indeed, but not a delight, and to be dismissed as quickly as may be.

3. The selfish way—when the real motive is to consume the coveted blessing upon ourselves—in some way to promote our own selfish advantage or pleasure.

4. The impulsive way—praying as feeling prompts, and when we feel so inclined—without any definite plan of prayer in our lives, or devout habit.

5. The faithless way—with no real dependence on the promises of God, or confident expectation of receiving what we ask or seek.

6. On the contrary, there is the thoughtful way, seeking to meditate upon God and intelligently understand both the nature of prayer and the good we seek.

7. The earnest way—with the attention of the mind and the desire of the heart absorbed in asking, with a determination to persevere.

8. The trustful way—coming in the spirit of a child; first believing that God's promises justify prayer, and then that we are coming to a Father, both able and willing.

9. The consistent way—that is, living as we pray, and so walking with God as to be in the way of blessing, and by fellowship with God inviting it.

10. The spiritual way—so cultivating acquaintance with the Holy Spirit that He can and does breathe in us first the desires we breathe out in prayer.

It is easy to see why we so often fail, and how we may succeed.—Missionary Review.

Argo Red Salmon is not only Pure Food, but it is the cheapest and most nutritious food in the country.

DANDRUFF

is a form of skin disease peculiar to the scalp. Properly treated it is as easily cured as any other skin trouble, but you must have an agent that will not only kill the germ and assist nature in healing the sores, but will lift the scales and tiny germs from the pores and chambers of the skin so that the surface shall be clear for nature's action.

Tetterine does all this; it not only kills the germs but breaks up the cake-like formation on the scalp and leads to a permanent cure. Try it.

Tetterine is an unequaled remedy for eczema, pimples, tetter, ringworm and other skin diseases. 50c. at your drug store or by mail on receipt of price. Shuptrine Co., Savannah, Ga.

SPRING TIME.

The time for gardening is here and you need garden tools. We can supply you at lowest prices.

Poultry Wire.

The best assorted stock in the county. Four different styles and weight.

Come and See.

Remember plumbing and bath room fixtures, a speciality. You will find us on Davis St. third door from Post office.

BURLINGTON HARDWARE CO.

RALEIGH AND SOUTHPORT RAILWAY COMPANY.

Southbound—daily.		STATIONS.		Northbound	
P. M.	A. M.			A. M.	P. M.
1:30	6:00	LvRaleighT t Ar.		9:25	4:30
1:40	6:11	Caraleigh	t	9:10	4:20
1.44	6:19	Sylvaola		9:01	4:15
1:50	6:25	Barnes		8:33	4:07
1:57	6:32	Hobby		8:45	4:00
2:05	6:42	McCullers		t 8.40	3:56
2:10	6:47	Banks		t 8:31	3:50
2.20	7:00	Willow Springs	t8:20	3:40
2:28	7.10	Cardenas		8:10	3:33
2:33	7:13	Varina	t	8:05	3:30
2:43	7:23	Fuquay Springs	8.00	3:20
2:50	7:30	Rawles		7:46	3:13
2:57	7:40	Chalybeate		7:40	3:07
3.02	7:45	Kipling		7:35	3:02
3:15	8:00	Cape Fear		7:20	2:46
3:21	8:08	Lillington		7:15	2:41
4:30	9:25	ArFayettevilleLv	6:00	1:30
		SUNDAY TRAINS.			
1:44	6:16	Sylvaola		9:01	4:15
1:50	6:25	Barnes		8:53	4:07
4:25	8:05	Raleigh		10:45	7:40
5:07	8:47	McCullers		10:00	7:00
5:25	9:05	Willow Springs	9:40	6:40
5:38	9:18	Varina		9:35	6:28
5:48	9:28	Fuquay Springs	9:28	6:20
6:03	9:43	Chalybeate		9:10	6:03
6:09	9:48	Kipling		9:05	5:55
6:30	10.00	Lillington		8:45	5:35
7:45	11:25	Fayetteville		7:30	4:20

JNO. A. MILLS, Pres. and Gen. Mgr.

Ask your grocer for Argo Red Salmon, and do not accept any substitute. There is no finer Salmon packed.

The grocers are handling Argo Red Salmon because it takes no argument to sell it, and the customers come back for more.

DIED.

Brazzle.

Stephen William Brazzle, aged three months, died July 13, 1908. He who said while on earth, "Suffer little children to come unto me" has taken this little one unto himself.

Funeral services at the home by the writer,

R. H. Peel.

Holland.

Agnes Hortense Holland, only child of Mr. C. W. Holland and wife, was born Oct. 21, 1907, died June 23, 1908. Only a few months did she remain in the earthly home, but the home ties have been broken by death and father and mother are saddened by her departure. Funeral services were conducted by the writer at Central Hill Baptist Church.

R. H. Peel.

Laine.

Miss Lillie W. Laine died June 27, 1908, aged twenty-three years. She had been a member of Barrett's Christian Church for several years and expressed herself before her death as ready to depart from earth to be with Jesus. Funeral services were conducted by the writer in the presence of friends who were saddened by her early death. May the Lord comfort the sorrowing parents and friends.

R. H. Peel.

Oberry.

Mrs. Sarah A. Oberry departed this life July 23, 1908, aged 68 years. She had been a member of Antioch Christian Church about 50 years, and gave testimony in both word and deed of a Christian life.

She leaves one daughter and a host of friends who are saddened by her death. Funeral services were conducted at Antioch Christian Church in the presence of a large gathering of friends. Services by the writer.

R. H. Peel.

Taylor.

Edward, the nine-month-old son of Mr. and Mrs. W. E. Taylor, died at their home in Liberty St., South Norfolk, Va., July 30, 1908. Funeral services conducted by the writer from the residence July 31, and the remains laid away in Magnolia Cemetery.

"As the sweet flower that scents the morn,

But withers in the rising day,

Thus lovely was this infant's dawn,

Thus swiftly fled its life away."

Our hearts go out in sympathy for the grief stricken parents. May the grace of God comfort and sustain them. July 31, 1908.

J. O. Cox.

Eley.

Hylah Darden, the eleven-month-old daughter of Mr. and Mrs. L. P. Eley, died at their home in Jackson St., South Norfolk, Va., July 25, 1908. She had been in delicate health almost all her life but for the past few weeks had been gaining rapidly, and was especially playful on the day before the end came; no sign of sickness was noticed until ten thirty on Friday night and she died about nine o'clock the next morning. The poet has truthfully said:—

"There is a reaper whose name is Death,

And with his sickle keen

He reaps the bearded grain at a breath,

And the flowers that grow between.

And the mother gave, in tears and pain,

The flowers she most did love;

She knew she would see them all again

In the fields of light above."

Funeral services were conducted from the residence by the writer Sunday afternoon, July 26, and the little lifeless form tenderly laid away in Magnolia Cemetery. A pastor's sympathy is extended to the sorrowing parents.

J. O. Cox.

Elder.

Whereas, it has pleased our gracious Heavenly Father to remove from labor and suffering to reward and peace, our much beloved Bro. W. W. Elder, and whereas, he was a devoted and most faithful member of Noon Day Christian Church, therefore be it resolved:

1. That while we bow in humble submission to the will of Him who makes no mistakes, we cannot cease mourning because of our loss in the death of Bro. Elder, who was one of our very best and most appreciated members.

2. That we commemorate the pious life of our departed friend and brother, extol his virtues and render thanks to Almighty God for his example in a faithful Christian life, and his honorable and upright citizenship, and pray the good Lord to comfort the broken hearted wife and children, and to enable them to submit, with pious resignation, to the will of an alwise Providence.

3. That a copy of these resolutions be sent to the bereaved family, as a token of our deep sympathy, a copy be sent to the Christian Sun for publication and a copy be recorded in our church register.

J. J. Fields,

J. W. Payne,

C. C. Huey.

TEACHER TRAINING THE SUNDAY SCHOOL'S GREATEST PROBLEM.

There are more than a million Sunday school teachers in the United States and Canada. In the wide outreach of their influence in Bible Study, they come in contact with 15,000,000 members of the Sunday schools of the international field. "More and more our church leaders recognize that teacher training is the Sunday school's greatest problem. Never were they so united in the determination to find its solution. Upon the result of their labors in this direction depends the largest success of all Sunday school work."

In its work of helpful service for the individual Sunday school, the International Sunday School Association maintains a Teacher Training Department, for the instruction and inspiration of the teachers in methods and work of teaching. In the development of its plans, it has established standards for two courses of study for teachers—one known as "First" and the other as "Advanced." International diplomas are given to those completing these studies.

At the Triennial Convention of the International Sunday School Association, 48 associations represented 6,704 teacher training classes, 79,086 students and 10,016 graduates. The largest number of students enrolled during the triennium in any single association was in Pennsylvania, which enrolled 14,268. Several denominations are now doing teacher training work, whose enrollments are equal to those of the International Association, and at the present time 61 state or provincial Sunday school associations have either especially appointed teacher training superintendents, or teacher training committees, to supervise this department of work.

During the past triennium the Teacher Training Department has been ably conducted by Mr. W. C. Pearce, of Chicago, who has been known as the International Teacher Training Superintendent. For more than a year he has had in addition to this work, the duties of the establishment of the Adult Department, which has grown with remarkable rapidity and strength. At the recent International Sunday School Convention at Louisville, Ky., Mr. Pearce was re-elected Adult Department Superintendent, to give his entire time to that work.

The duty of recommending a suitable person as Teacher Training Superintendent devolved upon a special committee of which Prof. H. M. Hamill, D.D., of Nashville, Tenn., Superintendent of Training work of the Methodist Episcopal Church, South, and chairman of the International Committee on Education, was chairman. In his absence, on account of illness, from the session of the Central Committee at Louisville the report of the special committee was presented by W. A. Eudaly, Esq., of Cincinnati, who recommended for the committee the name of Rev. Franklin McElfresh, A.M., D.D., Ph.D. (Ohio Wesleyan), of Columbus, Ohio, and he was unanimously elected Superintendent of the Teacher Training Department of the International Sunday School Association for the ensuing triennium.

Dr. McElfresh is now closing his sixth year as district superintendent of the Zanesville District Ohio Conference of the M. E. Church. He is a "Buckeye" by birth and education and graduate of the Ohio Wesleyan University, Delaware, Ohio. Post-graduate work in this institution earned for him the degree Ph.D., and the university later conferred upon him the honorary degree D.D. Activity in literary work, and a close and continued identification with educational and college life, have made him the educational leader of his own conference, as one of the strong educational pastors of Methodism. He is a member of a college fraternity chapter at Delaware with Bishop Anderson and Dr. Charles E. Jefferson of New York City.

Dr. McElfresh's interest in Christianity has been kingdom-wide, and his fraternal relations with all denominations have won for him their respect and love. He is a vigorous manly man in middle life, a man of culture and fine social qualities, a strong, original, thoughtful and pleasing platform speaker, with a rich voice of unusual forensic quality. He is equal to any demand that may be made upon him in presenting the educational side of Sunday school work before colleges, seminaries and conventions, and educational and ministerial gatherings.

Dr. McElfresh is a man of devotion and piety, of the manly type, and keeps close to the spiritual side of the work. During the summer months he will acquaint himself with his new duties as opportunity offers, will close his term as district superintendent and will officially assume his new office October 1.

POPUAR EXCURSION TO NORFOLK, VA. ,AUGUST 18th, 1908.

Southern Railway will opearte its popular excursion to Norfolk on August 18th. Train consists of first class day coaches and Pullman cars, giving two days and one night in Norfolk.

Following round trip rate from Elon College, $3.50.

For detailed information see large flyers, or call on your depot agent.

R. L. Vernon, Trav. Pass. Agent.

SEVERAL MEETINGS.

On the second Sunday in July I went to Girard to assist Rev. J. W. Elder in revival services. At the beginning of the meeting congregations were small and interest poor, but after a few days of hard labor the congregations and interest in the services increased greatly. The meeting continued until Wednesday night after the third Sunday. The church was greatly revived, and five were added to the membership. It was a pleasure to labor with this people.

On Saturday before the fourth Sunday of last month we began our meeting at Christiana. Rev. G. O. Lankford was with us and did the preaching. We feel that much good has resulted from this meeting. The Holy Spirit was present in great power. Men confessed their wrongs one to another, the church was deeply stirred and spiritually revived. At the close of the meeting seventeen had united with the church. Because of this meeting we thank God and take courage.

At present I am at Pleasant Grove with Bro. Lankford. Much interest is being manifested in the services. So far no members have been received.

Next week I go to Rock Springs to begin our meeting there.

May the Lord give us many precious souls during this revival season. The harvest is white and we need more consecrated workers.

Success to the Editor and the Sun family.

Fraternally,
J. H. Milam.

August 4, 1908.

Deafness Cannot be Cured
by local applications, as they cannot reach the diseased portion of the ear. There is only one way to cure deafness, and that is by constitutional remedies. Deafness is caused by an inflamed condition of the mucous lining of the Eustachian Tube. When this tube is inflamed you have a rumbling sound or imperfect hearing, and when it is entirely closed, Deafness is the result, and unless the inflammation can be taken out and this tube restored to its normal condition, hearing will be destroyed forever; nine cases out of ten are caused by Catarrh, which is nothing but an inflamed condition of the mucous surfaces.

We will give One Hundred Dollars for any case of deafness (caused by Catarrh) that cannot be cured by Hall's Catarrh Cure. Send for circulars free.

F. J. CHENEY & CO., Toledo, O.
Sold by Druggists, 75c.

TO CURE ECZEMA.

The one infallible method by which Eczema can be quickly and permanently cured is by the use of HEISKELL'S OINTMENT. For half a century this great remedy has been the means of curing skin diseases of every nature. Erysipelas, Tetter, Ulcers, Pimples, Ringworm, Biotchy Skin, Eruptions, Rough Skin, Salt Rheum, Scald Head—all yield as readily to the marvelous curative virtues of HEISKELL'S OINTMENT as the dread disease—Eczema. Before applying the ointment, bathe the affected parts, using HEISKELL'S MEDICINAL SOAP. HEISKELL'S BLOOD AND LIVER PILLS tone up the liver and cleanse the blood. Ointment, 50 cents a box; Soap, 25 cents a cake; Pills, 25 cents a bottle—at all druggists. Send for interesting book of testimonials to JOHNSTON, HOLLOWAY & Co., 531 Commerce Street, Philadelphia, Pa.

NEWS ITEMS.

Harry K. Thaw, murderer of Stanford White, has gone into bankruptcy, his assets being, as published, $128,012.38, liabilities $453,140.43.

The North Carolina Yearly Meeting of Friends (Quakers) has been in 209th annual session at Guilford College past week, many prominent Friends from this and other States being present.

The German government has given Count Zeppelin a check for $125,000 for his services, covering several years, in behalf of aerial navigation. It is believed the Count is about to bring to success his invention of a real airship, though he has met, and is likely yet to meet, many reverses.

Judge Broderick, of Ohio, has ruled that "The cigarette habit is just as bad as the liquor habit, and habitual drunkenness is always cause for divorce." So the young wife who testified in his court that her husband was accustomed to get up in the night to smoke cigarettes was granted a divorce.

A contemporary finds that the forty-five minutes of continued yelling at Chicago and the eighty-five minutes yelling at Denver when the candidates for the presidency were being named has many parallels and precedents in history, one of which in particular was the yelling of the Ephesians, "Great is Diana of the Ephesians," which lasted about the space of two hours. Maybe our modern political conventions will yet be able to equal the large lunged Ephesians. Who knows?

The Christian Sun is anxious for subscriptions and will go a long way to get them, but we give under before the esteemed Mocksville Record, which anxious contemporary importunes as follows: "Will we take eggs on subscription? We'll take the entire output of the hennery for the nex six months an pay for it in subscriptions. We'll take lye soap, clean rags, ginseng, pant patches, old bones, wood, green hides, hound pups, old clothes, lumber, cull ties, wagon tires, peanuts, stick candy, onions, crackers, turnip greens, sausage, town lots, cabbage leaf cigars, yearlings or milch cows, sorghum, pumpkins, spring mules, well seasoned shoats, sofa pillows, footstools, bachelor buttons, patent medicines, eight day clocks, patent churns, home-made sox, choice scrap iron, old maids and chewing gum. You can bring them by the wagon load, armful, in tow sacks, by the yard, gallon, or ton, in droves, swarms or schools. Yes, we'll take them. We'll take anything to get you to subscribe."

CPSIA information can be obtained
at www.ICGtesting.com
Printed in the USA
BVHW070804261218
536333BV00014B/2406/P